EXPLORING THE ELEMENTS

Chlorine

Jeff Mapua

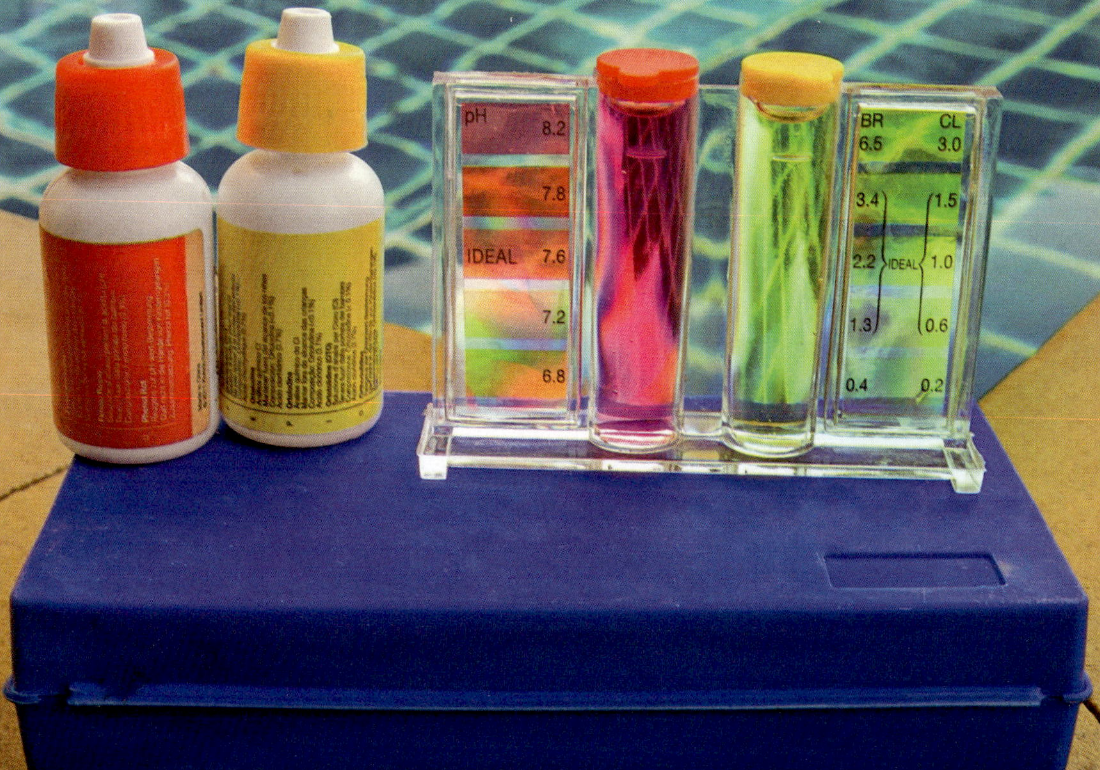

Enslow Publishing
101 W. 23rd Street
Suite 240
New York, NY 10011
USA
enslow.com

Published in 2019 by Enslow Publishing, LLC.
101 W. 23rd Street, Suite 240, New York, NY 10011

Library of Congress Cataloging-in-Publication Data
Names: Mapua, Jeff, author.
Title: Chlorine / Jeff Mapua.
Description: New York : Enslow Publishing, [2019] | Series: Exploring the elements | Audience: Grades 5 to 8. | Includes bibliographical references and index.
Identifiers: LCCN 2018006914 | ISBN 9781978503632 (library bound) | ISBN 9781978505384 (pbk.)
Subjects: LCSH: Chlorine—Juvenile literature. | Chemical elements—Juvenile literature.
Classification: LCC QD181.C5 M338 2018 | DDC 546/.732—dc23
LC record available at https://lccn.loc.gov/2018006914

Printed in the United States of America

To Our Readers: We have done our best to make sure all website addresses in this book were active and appropriate when we went to press. However, the author and the publisher have no control over and assume no liability for the material available on those websites or on any websites they may link to. Any comments or suggestions can be sent by email to customerservice@enslow.com.

Photo Credits: Cover, p. 1 (chemical element symbols) Jason Winter/Shutterstock.com; cover, p. 1 (pool and chemicals) oneSHUTTER oneMEMORY/Shutterstock.com; p. 8 udaix/Shutterstock.com; p. 11 ShadeDesign/Shutterstock.com; p. 13 Designua/Shutterstock.com; p. 16 Alexander A. Nedviga/Shutterstock.com; p. 17 julie deshaies/Shutterstock.com; p. 18 yaruna/Shutterstock.com; p. 21 Inna Bigun/Shutterstock.com; p. 23 photoiconix/Shutterstock.com; p. 25 Livre Partida/Shutterstock.com; p. 28 Universal History Archive /Universal Images Group/Getty Images; p. 29 AlexLMX/Shutterstock.com; p. 30 Franck Boston/Shutterstock.com; p. 36 Cmspic/Shutterstock.com; p. 38 MsMaria/Shutterstock.com; p. 40 Robert Hoetink/Shutterstock.com.

Contents

Introduction

Chlorine is one of the most beneficial chemical elements for humans. It is used to make swimming pools safe and help keep surfaces in hospitals clean. People have found ways to make food safer to eat and this element is even found in some drugs that fight cancer.

But chlorine is not just a chemical that people make. It is found in living organisms. More than 3,500 naturally occurring chlorinated organic compounds have been found. One of those organic compounds is called epibatidine. It is a naturally occurring compound found in a frog species found in Ecuador. When scientists studied the compound, they were surprised to see what they discovered.

The scientists found that the frog produced a toxin that acted like a pain-killer in mice. Not only did the toxin provide pain relief, but it was 200 times more powerful than the best known product available. It was an amazing discovery that could help people all around the world.

A toxin is a poisonous substance produced by a living organism. The frog that the scientists were studying was called the *Epipedobates tricolor*, or more commonly known as the phantasmal poison frog. It is sometimes called the candy cane frog due to its distinctive red and white stripes, although the color may vary from brown to red, and from white to yellow. The poison frog is one of several types of frog used by hunters who used their toxins to paralyze or kill animals. By rubbing their blow dart tips on the frog's skin, they were able to kill animals hundreds of times larger than the frog. The phantasmal poison frog produces around 80 different toxins on its skin. It was most likely a shocking surprise to scientists when they discovered that one of these toxins held medical uses for people.

The beneficial toxin was named epibatidine. There was one chlorine atom in the compound, and scientists remarked how similar its chemical structure resembled nicotine. Nicotine is another natural chemical compound with pain relief properties.

There was a significant barrier to conducting further studies of the frog, however. Because it was an endangered species, scientists could not gather enough of the toxin to study. So the small sample that they had was frozen to be studied at a later date when they may be able to continue their research. Luckily, new methods were invented to study the small amount of sample that they had.

Laboratories began making their own epibatidine. Upon further research, they discovered that it was too dangerous to be used as a drug for pain relief. Medical chemists and pharmacologists who study medicines continue to study the toxin to see if they could make it safe for people to take.

Dr. John Daly of the US National Institutes of Health believes that understanding the phantasmal poison frog's toxin could one day lead to a way to relieve the suffering caused by long-term pain in people. For now, large doses of epibatidine is fatal to humans. One day it could become safe for people, and become just another one of the many uses for chlorine.

1

The Story of Chlorine

Pesticides such as DDT and other chemicals made from chlorine can be harmful to people and animals. Chlorine is not always dangerous, and many beneficial, or useful, chlorine-containing substances are found in nature.

Building Compounds with Elements

Chlorine is an element. Elements are substances that contain a single kind of atom. The element iron (Fe) can be made into a nail, but if you cut the iron nail in half, it is still the element iron. If you continue to cut the nail until it is so small that you can barely see it, you still are going to be holding the element iron. Even if you were able to cut the nail down to the size of a single atom, you would still have the element iron.

Elements, Compounds, and Mixtures

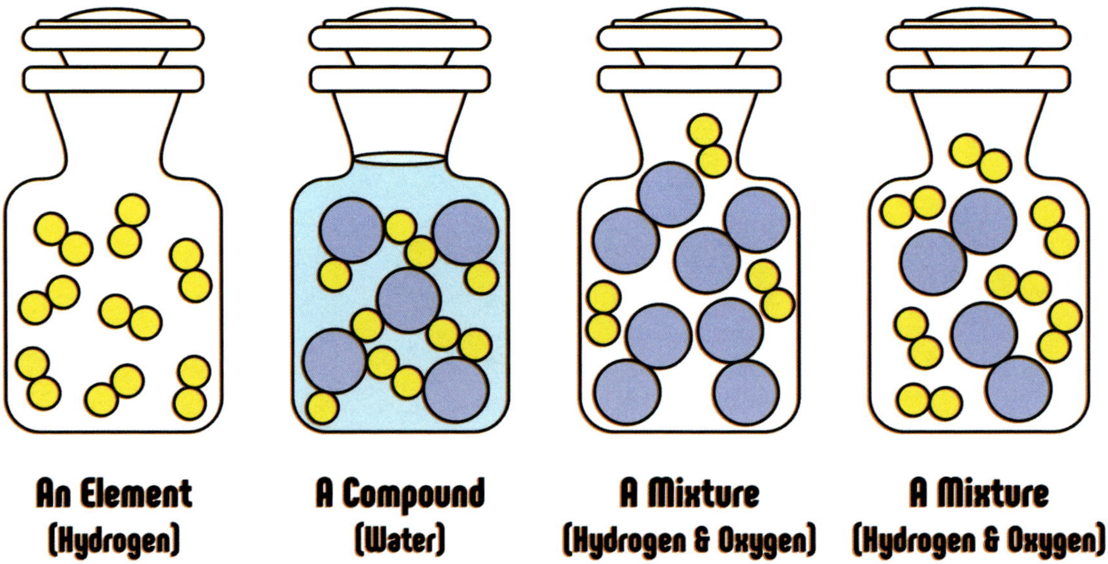

A compound is a substance formed by combining two elements chemically. A mixture implies two substances becoming one physically.

If you combined the iron atom with an atom of another element, then it would form a compound. Compounds occur when two or more different elements combine. Rust is a compound made of the elements iron and oxygen (O).

In nature, chlorine is too reactive to exist in a pure elemental form. It exists only in compounds. Chlorine was first discovered by a scientist who was experimenting with various compounds.

Mistaken Identity

In 1774, Swedish chemist Carl Wilhelm Scheele (1742–1786) mixed a shiny mineral with a liquid compound he called *spiritus salis*. A sharp-smelling, yellowish-green gas poured out of the mixture. Scheele wrote in his notes that the experiment created a "suffocating smell, which was most oppressive to the lungs."

Scheele continued to experiment with this gas. It dissolved some metals and caused red flower petals to turn white. Despite the gas's special properties, Scheele was not sure whether he had identified a new element. He thought the mysterious substance might be a compound containing the element oxygen (O).

More than thirty years later in 1810, an English chemist named Humphry Davy began conducting tests on the gas. Davy wanted to test Scheele's theory to see whether the gas contained oxygen.

Sir Humphry Davy 1778–1829

In addition to proving that chlorine was a single element, Humphry Davy identified the elements potassium (K), sodium (Na), magnesium (Mg), calcium (Ca), strontium (Sr), barium (Ba), and iodine (I). He also invented a special helmet lamp for coal miners.

At 34, Humphry Davy was such a successful scientist that the British royal family decided to make him a knight. Unfortunately for Davy, all the scientific experiments and the glory he received came at a price. The same year he identified chlorine as an element, a mixture of chemicals in Davy's lab exploded and temporarily blinded him.

He tried to extract oxygen from the gas, but he never could do it. After many more tests, Davy realized the gas was not a compound of oxygen at all. It was not even a compound—it was an element! Because of the gas's color, Davy named the element *chlorine*, from the Greek word *khloros*, meaning "greenish-yellow."

Building Blocks

In addition to its color and strong odor, chlorine has other properties that make it different from the rest of the elements. No two elements are exactly alike. Individual elements are different because the atoms they are made of are different.

Atoms are the basic building blocks of all matter. The atoms of an element combine with other atoms to form molecules. Chlorine atoms combine to create chlorine molecules. During Scheele and Davy's experiments with chlorine, they saw a greenish-yellow gas. This gas is made up of diatomic chlorine molecules. (*Diatomic* means "containing two atoms.") In chemical formulas that contain chlorine, you often see the diatomic form of chlorine written as Cl_2.

Until the twentieth century, the atom was the smallest known physical structure. Then physicists discovered that atoms are made up of even smaller parts. Known as subatomic particles, these are called protons, neutrons, and electrons. Scientists also discovered that atoms were held together by the electromagnetic attraction between subatomic particles. Protons have a positive electric

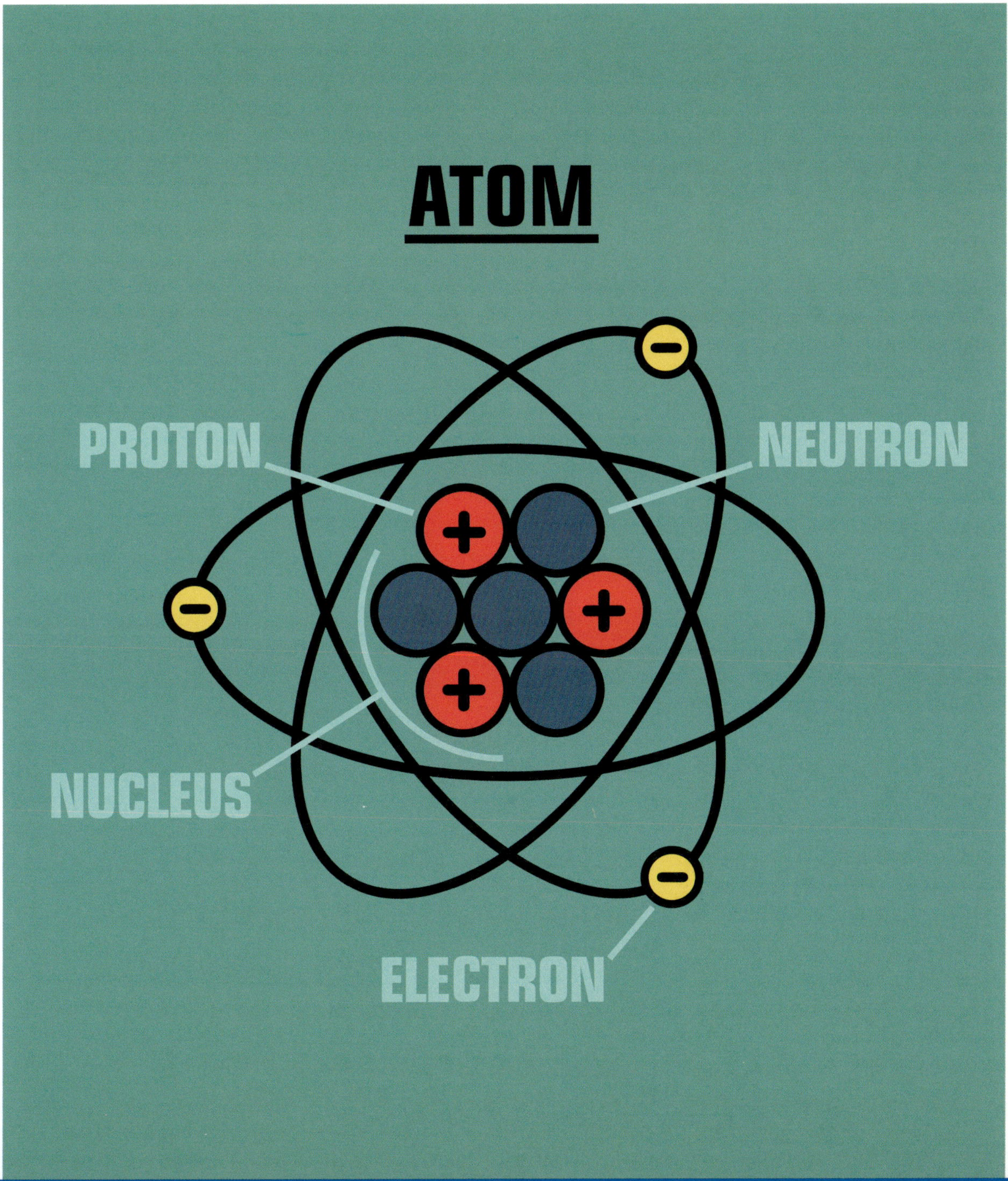

Atoms can be broken down into smaller parts; protons and neutrons make up the nucleus, while electrons orbit the nucleus.

charge; electrons have a negative electric charge. Neutrons, as their name indicates, are neutral, meaning they have no charge.

Inside the Atom

The protons, neutrons, and electrons in all atoms are exactly the same. It is the number and arrangement of these subatomic particles that makes an atom of one element different from the atoms of all other elements. All atoms have a core called a nucleus. The protons and neutrons are found inside this nucleus.

Chlorine atoms 1–2, and only chlorine atoms, have seventeen protons. The number of protons in an atom is called the atomic number, so chlorine's atomic number is 17. About 75 percent of chlorine atoms found in nature have eighteen neutrons (Chlorine-35), while about 25 percent contain twenty neutrons (Chlorine-37). Chlorine-35 and -37 are not different elements because they still contain the same number of protons (17). They are considered isotopes of chlorine.

Elements in the periodic table are organized according to their atomic numbers, or the number of protons in their nuclei. Each element has its own atomic number. The element with the lowest atomic number is hydrogen, with an atomic number of 1, and is located in the upper left-hand corner of the table. Presently, the element with the highest atomic number—ununoctium, atomic number 118—is located in the lower right-hand corner.

Chlorine's seventeen protons make it the seventeenth element on the periodic table.

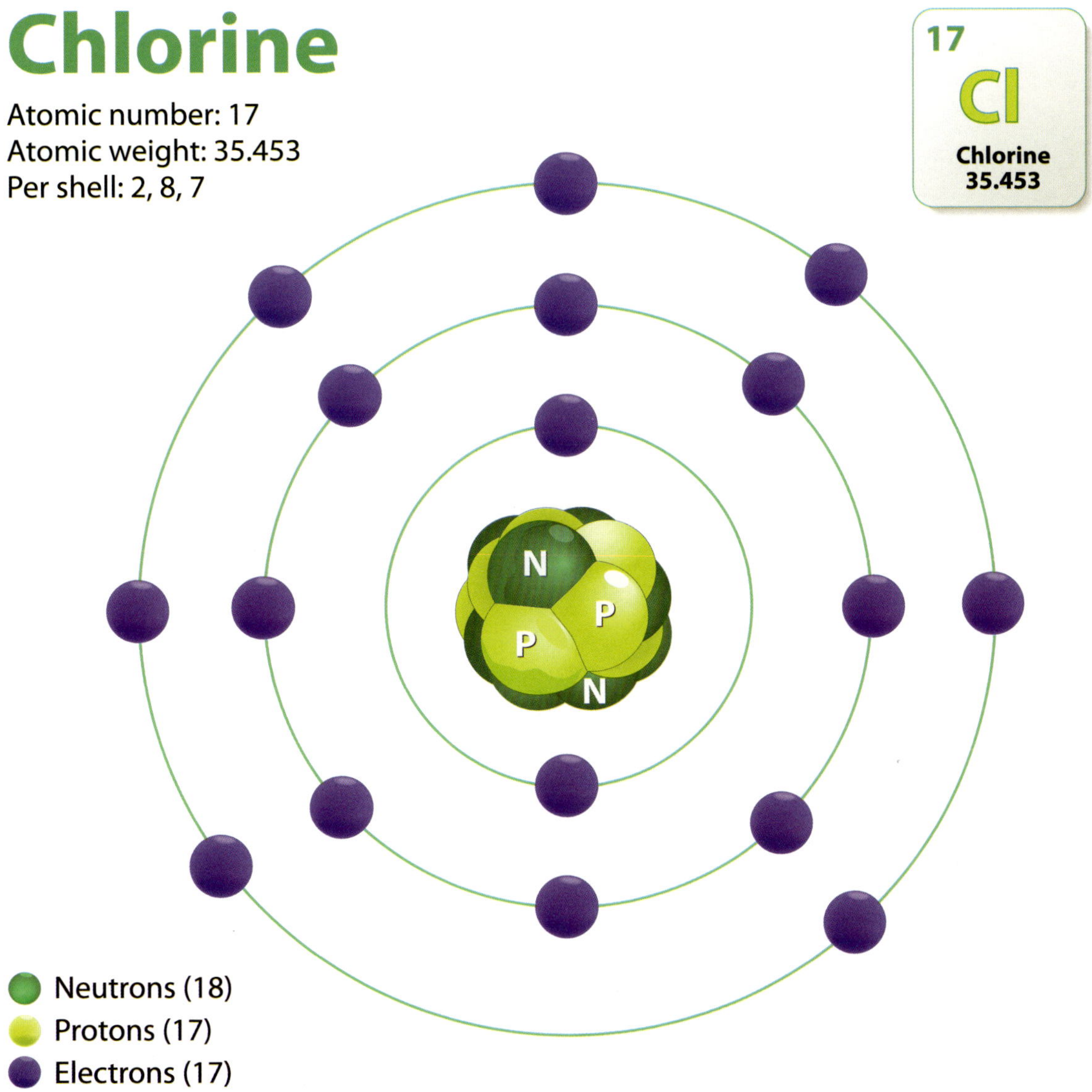

A chlorine atom, showing its seventeen electrons orbiting the nucleus.

An atom's electrons move around in shells that are located outside of the nucleus. An atom can have just one shell, or up to seven shells. For all elements, the rules for the shells are the same: The first shell can hold two electrons, the second shell can hold up to eight electrons. The third shell can hold thirty-two electrons, and the higher shells can hold even more. A chlorine atom has three shells. It has two electrons in its first shell, eight in its second, and seven in its third. Add these numbers, and you'll see that chlorine has seventeen total electrons.

The number of electrons in an atom's outer shell determines whether the atom is reactive or not reactive. For chlorine, its seven electrons in its outer shell make it very reactive with other elements. There are over 3,500 naturally occurring organic compounds with chlorine identified. Chlorine is usually found in compounds because it is so reactive.

It was chlorine's ability to react with other elements that interested Scheele and Davy. In the late 1800s, chlorine continued to inspire other scientists, including a chemist who forever changed how we look at elements.

2

Setting the Table

In the 1860s, a Russian chemist named Dmitry Mendeleev visited an enormous salt mine in Poland. He was fascinated by the elements found in the mine, including chlorine, sodium, bromine (Br), and potassium. He wondered how these elements could be in the same mine and how they behaved and reacted with each other.

Several years later, Mendeleev was teaching chemistry at the University of St. Petersburg in Russia, and wanted to create a better way for his students to study and remember the elements. He began thinking again about the properties of the different elements. He considered the atomic mass, or weight, of each known element. He created individual cards for each element and then arranged them in a horizontal row, according to their

Chlorine at a Glance

Chemical Symbol: Cl
Classification: nonmetal
Family: Halogens
Properties: Poisonous, greenish-yellow, water-soluble gas; highly reactive; occurs only in compounds in nature; not combustible, but will enable other elements to catch fire (oxidizing agent)
Discovered By: Carl Wilhelm Scheele, in 1774; confirmed as an element in 1810 by Sir Humphry Davy
Atomic Number: 17
Atomic Weight: 35.453 amu
Protons: 17
Electrons: 17
Neutrons: 18 (75%); 20 (25%)
Density of Solid: 3.2 g/cm3 at 0°C
Melting Point: –150.7°F (–101.5°C)
Boiling Point: –30.28°F (–34.4°C)
Commonly Found: In seawater and earth's crust

Chlorine is the 17th element on the periodic table of elements, part of the halogens.

atomic mass. Mendeleev knew the weights of hydrogen (the lightest) through uranium (the heaviest known at the time) and placed them accordingly. Mendeleev also knew that the elements had some predictable properties, and arranged the rows so elements with similar properties fell into the same columns. When arranged this way, his chart showed repeating patterns, or periods, among the properties of the elements. This new chart, which he published in 1869, became known as the periodic table of elements. Mendeleev's chart evolved into the periodic table we know today.

Mendeleev left empty spaces in his table where no element with suitable properties was known. Many of the elements predicted by Mendeleev have since been discovered and added to the table.

By Atomic Number and Periods

The modern periodic table takes Mendeleev's idea and makes it easier to understand. The original version arranged the elements according to weight, or atomic mass. Today's version arranges the elements by atomic number, which represents the number of protons in the nucleus of the atom. Like Mendeleev's table, the periodic table we use today also has horizontal rows called periods. In each period, the elements are arranged from the least to greatest atomic number, reading left to right. You'll find chlorine in the third period, on the right-hand side of the periodic table.

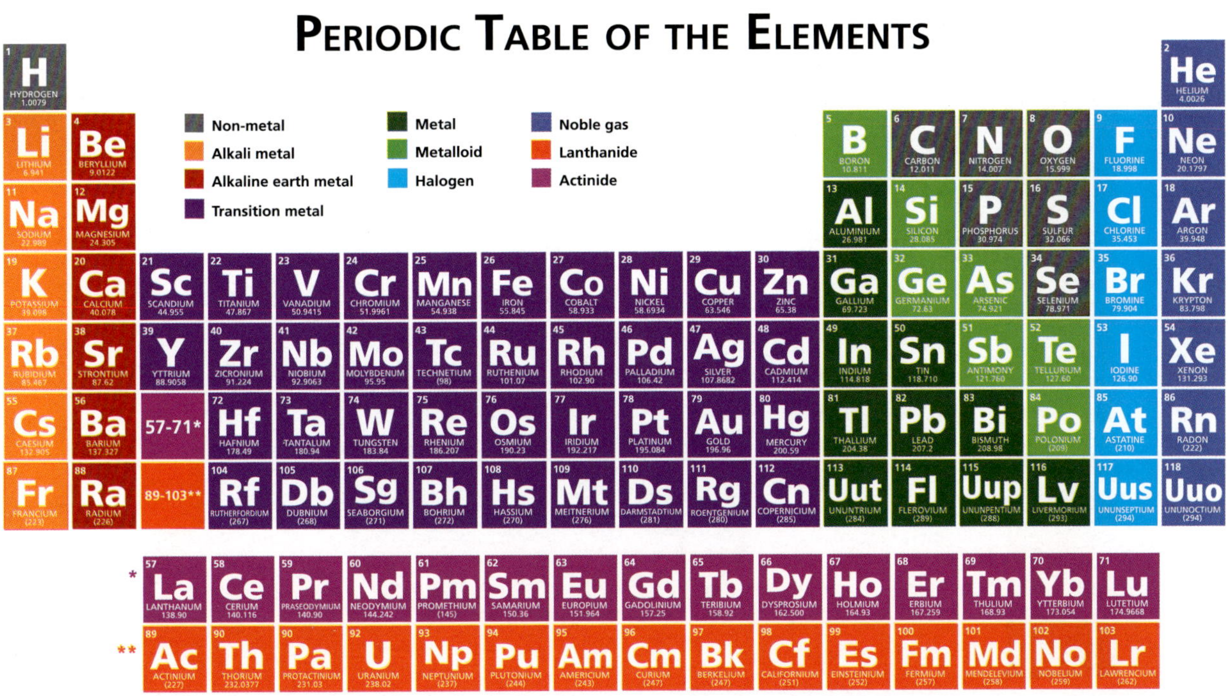

The periodic table of elements was first arranged by Dmitry Mendeleev, a Russian chemist and inventor.

In Groups

In addition to organizing elements by periods, the periodic table also arranges elements in groups. An element is assigned a group based on its chemical properties. Many properties are related to the number of electrons in the outermost shell of the element's atom.

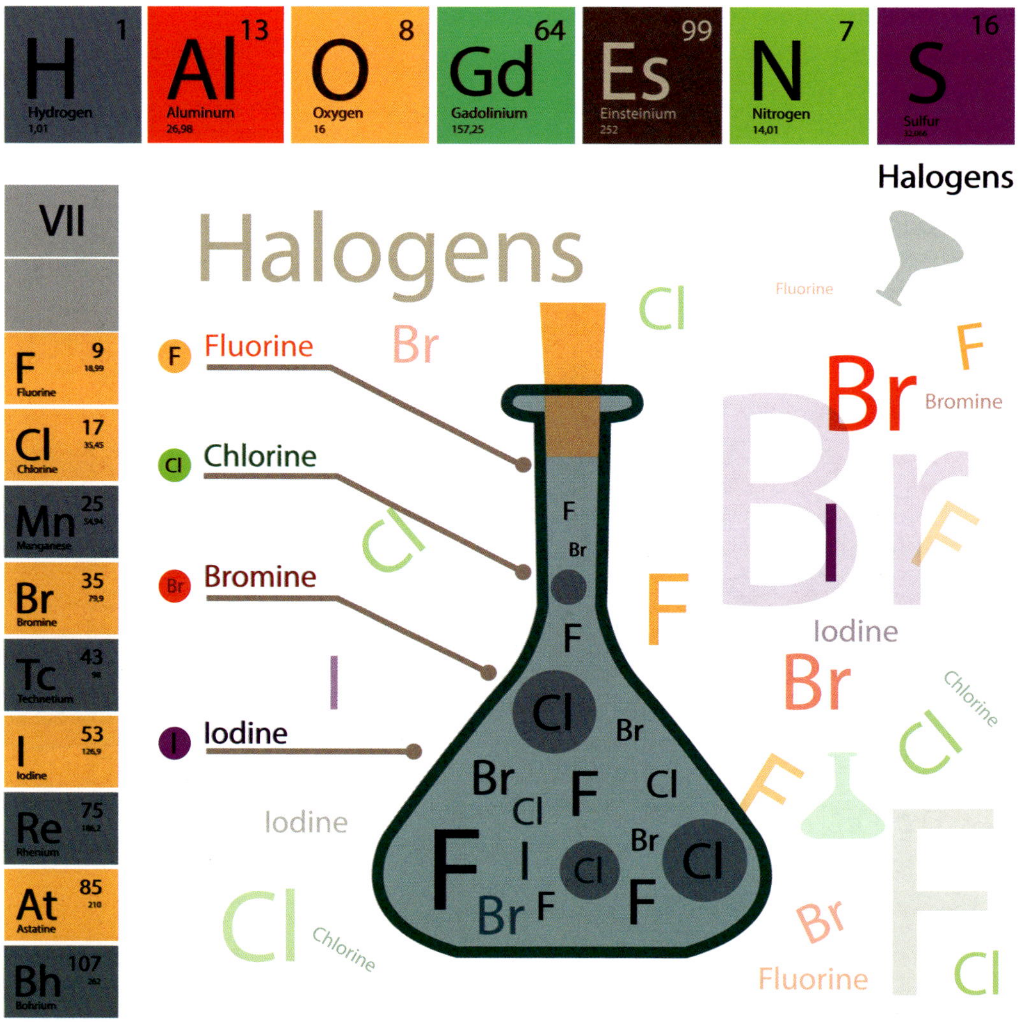

The halogens contain five chemically related elements: fluorine (F), chlorine (Cl), bromine (Br), iodine (I), and astatine (At).

Each group is assigned a number, 1 through 18, which appears above its column in the table. The groups are also identified by a Roman numeral and a letter, either A or B. Some tables include both labels. Elements in the A groups are known as representative elements. Chlorine is in an A group. Elements in the B groups, such as such as iron and copper (Cu), are all classified as metals.

The elements within a group are sometimes referred to as a family. Chlorine and the other elements belonging to group 17 (or VIIA), a family known as the halogens. This name means "salt formers." In chemical terms, a salt is formed when a metal atom replaces a hydrogen atom in an acid compound. Table salt, for example, is a salt called sodium chloride (NaCl). It is formed when the metal sodium (Na) replaces the hydrogen (H) in hydrochloric acid (HCl).

The first element in group 17 is fluorine (F), the most reactive element in the group. Reactive means that it will easily combine with other elements. Chlorine, which is also very reactive, is the second halogen. The other halogens are bromine, iodine, and astatine (At).

Halogens are nonmetals. Elements that are nonmetals are not good electrical conductors; nonmetals do not carry, or conduct, electricity well. Another property of some nonmetals is that they are not malleable, meaning they are not easily shaped into something else. Nonmetals can exist as gases like chlorine and as solids like sulfur (S).

3

Bonds and Compounds

The chemical behavior of atoms largely depends on electric charges. In particular, it is the arrangement of the negatively charged electrons that determines how elements react with one another. Remember that electrons circulate in shells. The number of electrons in an atom's outermost shell is crucial to its chemical behavior, for it is these electrons that allow an atom to create bonds with other atoms. Chemical bonds are either covalent or ionic.

Covalent Bonds

In a chlorine atom, seven of its seventeen total electrons are in its outermost (third) electron shell. The outermost shell is called the valence shell, so the seven electrons in it are called valence electrons. Chlorine's valence electrons allow it to form covalent bonds, which result when atoms share electrons.

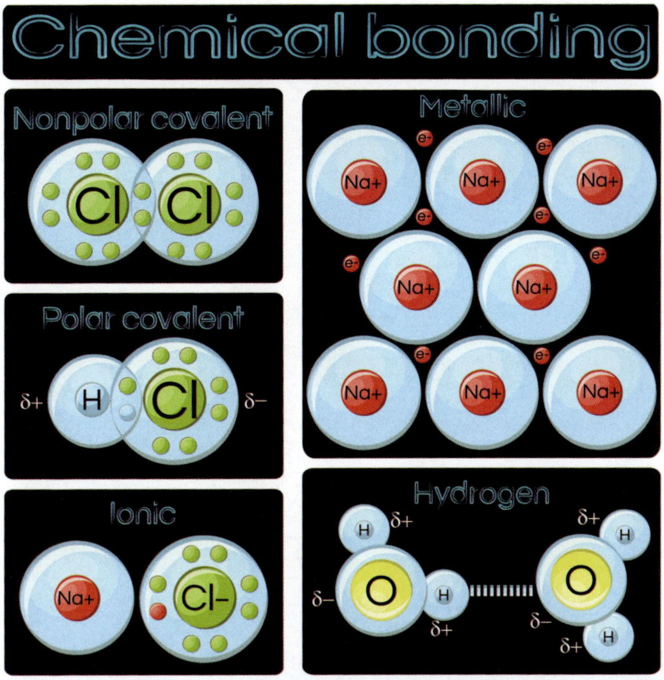

Types of chemical bonding include covalent and ionic.

Hydrogen chloride (HCl) is a molecule made up of one hydrogen atom and one chlorine atom. Hydrogen has one electron in its outer shell, which it tends to share with other atoms. Chlorine has seven electrons in its outer shell. When chlorine and hydrogen combine, hydrogen shares its one electron with chlorine. Chlorine then has eight electrons in its outer shell. This fills chlorine's outer shell, giving it a stable electron arrangement. At the same time, chlorine shares one of its electrons with the hydrogen atom. Hydrogen then has two electrons in its outer shell, making it full, too. By sharing electrons, both atoms get stable, filled outer shells.

Hydrogen chloride is an important molecule. Without it, you wouldn't be able to digest the food you eat. Inside your stomach is a weak form of hydrochloric acid, which is hydrogen chloride dissolved in water. The hydrochloric acid in your stomach breaks down food so that your body can absorb the proteins and other nutrients. This gives you energy to read this book, ride your bike, to live! Hydrogen chloride is just one of the many compounds of chlorine that our bodies rely on.

Ionic Bonds

If you've gone swimming in the ocean, you have been in the water with the compound sodium chloride (NaCl). This combination of sodium and chlorine gives seawater its salty taste. Sodium chloride is the chemical name for table salt, the seasoning you sprinkle on your food. Covalent bonds occur when atoms *share* one or more electrons. In the bond that holds together sodium chloride, one of the atoms *donates* one or more electrons to another element.

This type of bond works differently than covalent bonds. Sodium has one electron in its outermost shell. Under the right conditions, the neutrally charged sodium atom gives up this electron when it comes together with a chlorine atom. When the sodium atom loses an electron, it is left with a positive charge. A chlorine atom that gains an electron from sodium becomes negatively charged. As a result, the attraction between the positive sodium and the negative chlorine holds the two atoms together. Charged atoms are called ions, so this attraction is called an ionic bond.

Ionic Bonding of Sodium Chloride

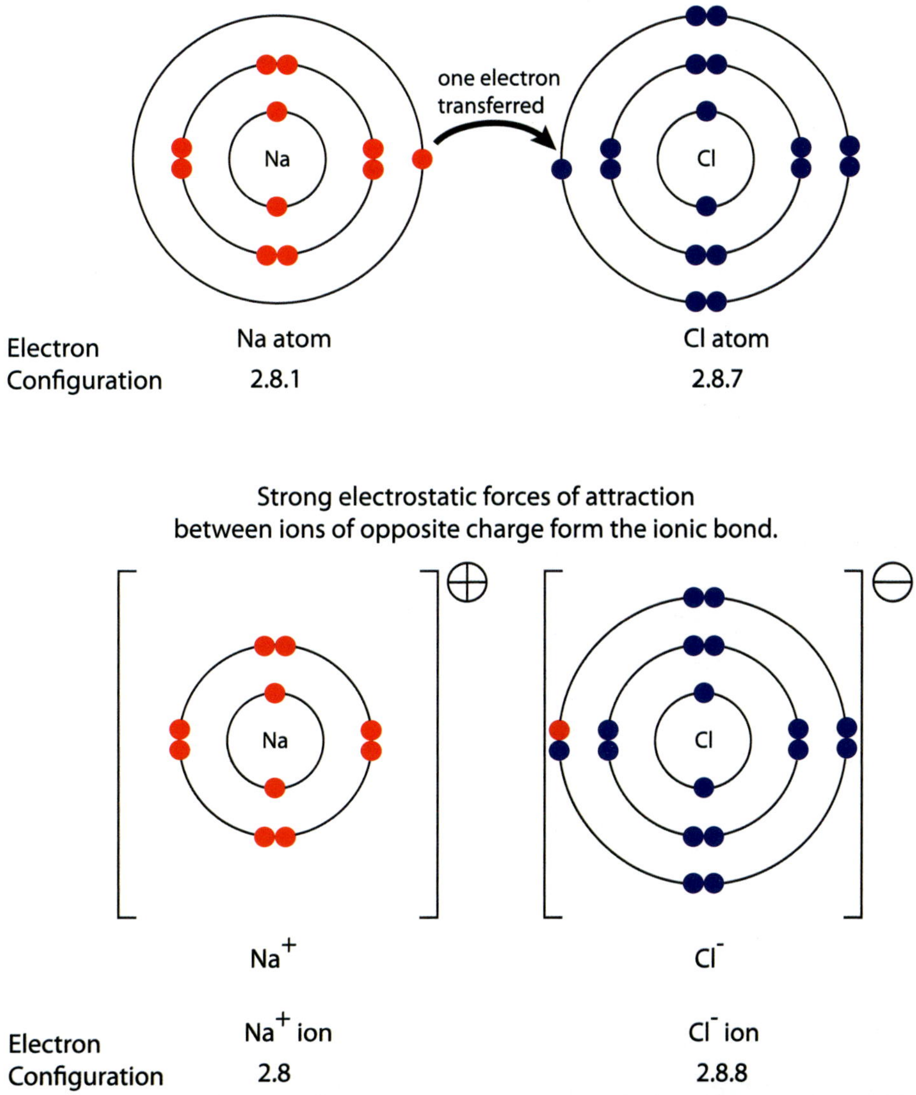

Ionic bonding involves an electrostatic attraction between oppositely charged ions.

Releasing Chlorine

Sodium chloride is an ionic compound made of sodium and chlorine. Scientists discovered that sodium chloride from seawater can be separated to produce chlorine gas. One common way this is done is by passing electricity through a container of seawater. This method, called electrolysis, separates the chloride ion atoms from the sodium ions.

The flow of electricity takes the electron away from the chloride ion and gives it back to the sodium ion. When electrons are removed, the chloride ions become chlorine atoms, which are released from the seawater as a gas. There are laboratories around the world that have huge vats, or tubs, of salt water that get zapped with electricity so that scientists can then collect the released chlorine gas.

Isotopes and Radioactivity

Chlorine-36 is a radioactive isotope formed when cosmic radiation from the solar system reacts with the earth's atmosphere. Isotopes are atoms that have the same number of protons but a different number of neutrons. Tiny amounts of chlorine-36 are found in our atmosphere, on the moon, and Mars. Chlorine-36 has a half-life of about 300,000 years. This means it will take about that long for half of this element to decay into a different element. When archeologists, geologists, and other scientists study something very old, they sometimes look for chlorine-36. If it is present, then they can measure the isotope's radioactivity to figure out about how old something is.

Producing Salt

In addition to electrolysis, scientists also use the remains of ancient oceans to produce chlorine. Deep inside the earth are giant pillars of salt called salt domes. Salt domes are made from the same salt that was in the oceans when dinosaurs existed. As the ocean water evaporated, the salt from the seawater was left behind, creating thick salt beds or flats. Over millions of years, these salt flats were covered by layers of sediment, dirt, and rock and ended up buried deep underground.

Sometimes this ancient salt appears on the earth's surface when it rises up through the groundwater and forms saltwater pools.

Salt crusts up on the shore of this pool, left behind when the water evaporates.

When you see brine pools far from the ocean, you know that an ancient salt bed must be underground. Underground salt can be mined by digging. Another method of collection is called solution mining. This requires long pipes to be inserted deep into the ground. One pipe pushes water into the ground until it reaches the salt. The salt and water then get mixed together, dissolving the salt and creating brine. Another pipe with a pump sucks up this salty mixture, or solution, to the earth's surface. The water is then evaporated from the solution, leaving behind salt.

Evaporation alone can be used to gather salt, too. In areas near seawater, like California, there are large ponds of salt water that have formed naturally or have been created by humans. A system of small dams helps to keep the salty water in one place so that the sun and wind can evaporate the water. The salt that is left behind is then harvested, more salt water is added, and the cycle starts all over again.

The methods described above produce the sodium chloride that is made into sea salt to season your food or chlorine to whiten your socks. In 2016, approximately 255 million metric tons of salt were produced in the world. Of that amount, China produced the most—more than 58 million tons.

4

Deadly Element

Chlorine is poisonous and can be deadly. During World War I, German chemists invented weapons using chlorine gas. The gas was pumped directly onto the battlefield using tanks and hoses, or could be delivered from above using special artillery shells. German soldiers used gas masks to protect them from inhaling it. If the wind was right, the greenish-yellow gas would blow over the enemy trenches. Just like the suffocating gas that Scheele and Davy experienced, this gas immediately started to damage the throats, lungs, and eyes of unprotected soldiers. Many were injured or killed.

Other forms of chlorine-based gases, such as deadly mustard gas, were used by many countries in World War II. As recently as 2016, chlorine-based gas weapons were used in the Syrian civil war. These gases had the ability to kill people almost instantly, or could kill very slowly and painfully. Once released, these gases also

Chlorine gas has been a deadly component in many wars, from World War I and recently in the Syrian civil war.

Creating Uut and Uup

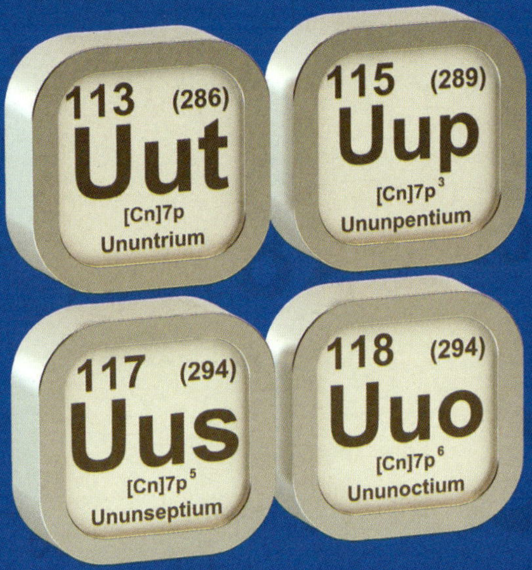

These oddly named elements are some of the most recent to have been created in the lab.

In January 2004, a team of American and Russian scientists announced they had created two new elements: ununtrium (Uut) and ununpentium (Uup). Within a few seconds of producing Uut and Uup, the scientists observed that the elements started to break down, or decay. In the blink of an eye, Uut and Uup had quickly changed from new elements into elements that were already known to exist.

Even though the scientists observed Uut and Uup, these elements were not automatically added to the periodic table. Instead, they were temporarily placed in the gaps at the bottom of the periodic table. Uut was element 113, and Uup was element 115. After scientists in Japan recreated the element in 2012, Uut was renamed nihonium. It was not until 2015 when Uup was recognized by the International Union of Pure and Applied Chemistry. It was then renamed moscovium.

Uut has an atomic weight of 284, and Uup has an atomic weight of 288. The relatively enormous atomic weights of these new elements led scientists to describe them as "superheavies." Even heavier elements have since been discovered including tennessine, element 117, and oganesson, element 118.

When chlorofluorocarbons encounter ozone, they form a new kind of chlorine, intensely harmful to the ozone layer of Earth.

poisoned birds, fish, and other animals that were unlucky enough to be in the vicinity. In 1925, a mere ten years after chlorine gas was first used as a weapon of war, more than 100 nations signed the Geneva Protocol. This agreement prohibited the use of "asphyxiating gas" and other such chemical weapons.

Harming the Ozone Layer

DDT and chlorine gases aren't the only ways that humans have tainted the environment with chlorine. Chlorofluorocarbons, or CFCs, are useful manufactured compounds made from chlorine, carbon, and fluorine. One type of CFC was found to be a very good coolant, so was widely used in refrigerators and air conditioners. CFCs in liquid form could be added to spray cans to act as a propellant for products such as air deodorizers and hairspray.

But in the 1970s, scientists started to realize that CFCs were eating away at the ozone layer that surrounds the Earth. The ozone layer of the atmosphere protects us from the sun's ultraviolet (UV) rays, which can damage eyes and cause skin cancer.

As you might guess, the ozone layer is made up of ozone molecules (O_3). When CFCs encounter ozone molecules, they change those ozone molecules into a form of chlorine. This new form of chlorine then reacts with other ozone molecules and changes them. So a single CFC molecule can destroy thousands of ozone molecules. When it became clear what was happening in the atmosphere, governments around the world began passing laws to ban the use of CFCs. The United States completely phased out the production of CFCs in 1996. Laws have helped to slow the damage to the ozone layer, but they can't entirely reverse the harm that already has been done.

Cancer-Causing Compounds

Polychlorinated biphenyls (PCBs) are another class of chlorine compounds that have harmed the environment. Beginning in 1929, these chemicals were used in everything from mascara to machinery. Similar to CFCs, PCBs were used to keep things cool and dissolve mixtures, and nearly every manufacturer across the globe used PCBs.

Unfortunately, as with CFCs, the miracle of PCBs was too good to be true. In the late 1970s, scientists discovered that PCBs caused cancer. Even worse, PCBs were hard to remove from the environment. Even if the harmful compounds were no longer produced, the PCBs already in the ground and in the water could still cause cancer in people and animals. Just like DDT, PCBs got into the rivers, streams, and lakes in America and started to make bald eagles sick. By 1977, the United States government banned the domestic production of PCBs.

Taken to the Cleaners

At one time, even your local dry cleaner used a dangerous chlorine compound. Carbon tetrachloride, or CCl_4 is a solvent, which means it can dissolve other substances. CCl_4 is so strong it can dissolve grease and oil. Dry-cleaning businesses used it to clean clothes that were too delicate to be washed with soap and water. Failure to dispose of this solvent properly resulted in polluted drinking water.

Think about how powerful this solvent has to be to break down grease. Then think about how delicate your liver, kidneys, and other organs are! As more people and the environment were exposed to CCl_4, scientists soon determined that it could be a deadly combination. Dry cleaners now use more environmentally safe cleaners.

5

A World with Chlorine

While some chlorine compounds are too dangerous to be used, many chlorine compounds are beneficial to humans. For example, chlorine is combined with other elements to create some types of plastic. Look around your house and you will find plastic in nearly every room. There are probably chlorine-containing plastic trash bags in your kitchen, plastic pipes attached to your bathroom sink, and a plastic remote control for your television.

Keeping Clean with Chlorine

You'll probably find chlorine in your laundry room, in the form of bleach. Sodium hypochlorite (NaOCl), or bleach, is a compound made from one atom of sodium (Na), one atom of oxygen (O), and one atom of chlorine (Cl).

Bleach might brighten your white clothes, but you still have to be careful when you use it. If spilled onto clothing you don't want whitened, like your jeans, you can end up with a bright white spot. If you get bleach on your skin or in your eyes it can burn. Non-chlorine bleach brightens with hydrogen peroxide instead of chlorine and doesn't strip the colors from fabrics. Non-chlorine bleaches are less damaging to the environment, too.

Swimming with Chlorine

If you've ever gone to a swimming pool, you've come into contact with sodium hypochlorite. Bleach is added to swimming pools to help prevent bacteria and algae from growing. If bleach were not added to a pool, clumps of green algae would begin to grow and it would be more like swimming in a pond!

Green algae are made up of living cells. When these cells come into contact with the sodium hypochlorite, a chemical reaction takes place. During the reaction, chlorine atoms replace the original atoms in the proteins of the cell membranes. This causes a change in the shape of the membranes and kills the algae.

Like algae, you also are made up of living cells. If you add too much bleach to the pool, it can harm your cells, causing your eyes and skin to feel itchy and dry.

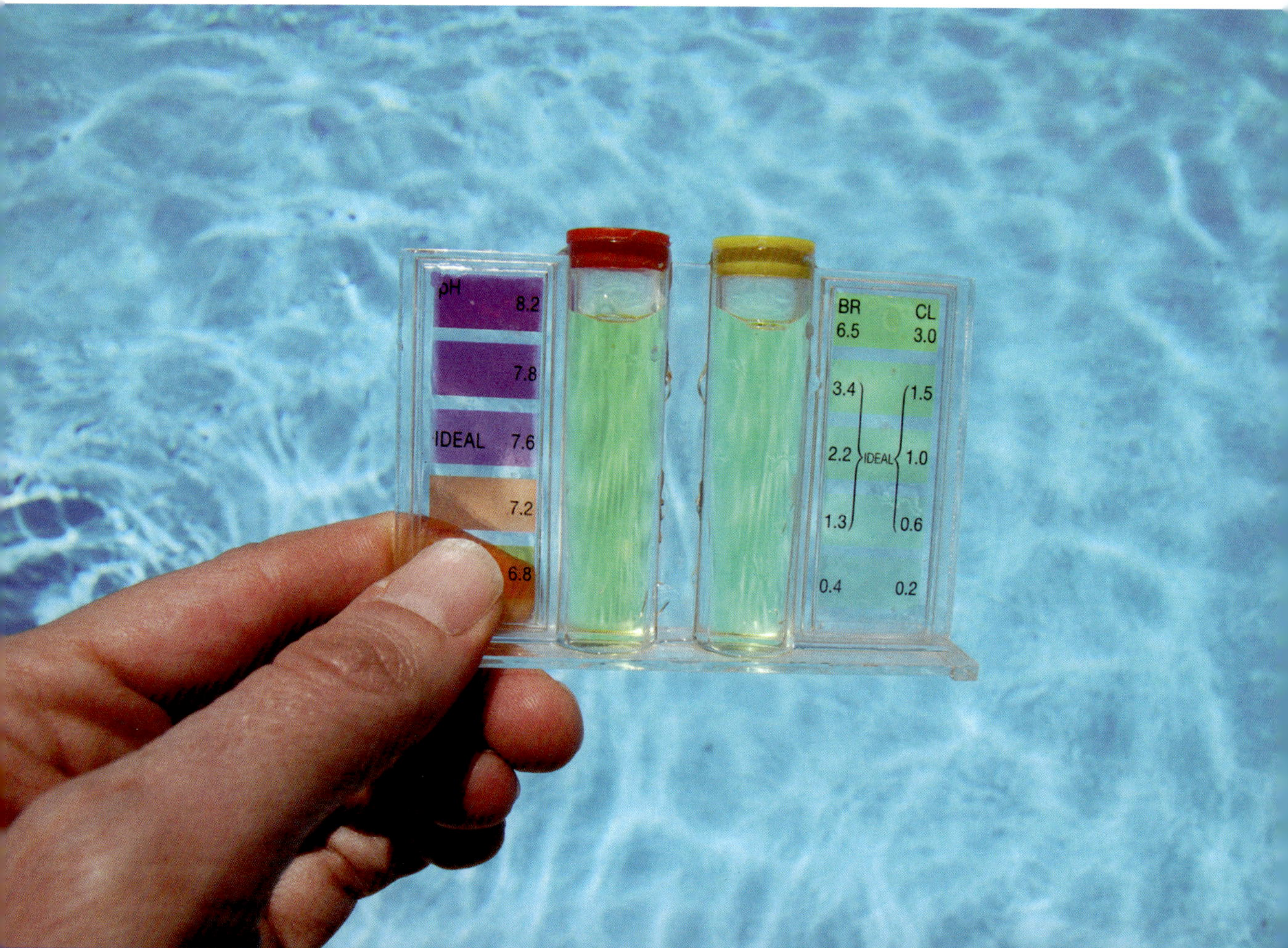

It's important to check the chemical levels in pools to ensure the water is safe for swimming.

Disinfectant bleach also is added to drinking water. Humans can suffer and even die when they drink water that has certain bacteria floating in it. In the early 1900s, for example, more than 25,000 people died from typhoid fever, a disease caused by bacteria.

To stop the spread of disease, chlorine was added to drinking water. The Chlorine Chemistry Council says that 98 percent of drinking water in the United States now has chlorine added to it. In other countries, deadly bacteria can thrive in some sources of drinking water. Governments and organizations are continuing to work together to bring chlorinated water to poorer nations.

Chlorine in the Kitchen

Humans have used sodium chloride (NaCl; table salt) for thousands of years. Some of the earliest books ever written tell about people using salt. In ancient kitchens, salt was used to preserve food so it would last longer. When fish or meat is covered in salt, the salt draws moisture out of the flesh. Without a moist environment, mold and other bacteria cannot grow, and so the meat does not spoil. Preserving food by salting is still done today.

Salt also is used to add extra flavor to foods. One of the reasons why we like the taste of salt

A Game of Chicken

In the United States, chickens are washed with a chlorine solution before being sold at market. The wash kills harmful bacteria including *Salmonella* and *Campylobacter*, and keeps people safe from eating contaminated food. The United Kingdom is considering importing this chicken from the US, though many people in the UK are afraid that chlorine is dangerous.

Scientists in both the US and UK say the amount of chlorine used to clean chickens is safe. The main concern is that the chlorine wash is a shortcut, and companies will skip other important steps to ensure food safety.

You've probably got chlorine in your kitchen, in the form of table salt!

is because we need it in order to be healthy. According to the Salt Institute, we all need about .28 percent of salt in our bodies to stay healthy. Having salt in our diet helps to keep the natural chemical balance inside our bodies. Too much salt in your diet can be a bad thing; an excess of salt can cause heart problems and other illnesses. Because salt is found naturally in many of the vegetables and meats we eat, it's best to limit salty snacks.

Road Salt for Safety

In its mineral form, sodium chloride, also called halite or rock salt, is used to clear roads of ice and snow.

For this reason, it is also called road salt. If you live in an area that has harsh winter weather, you'll often see trucks spreading road salt. Car tires crush the solid NaCl crystals, which then combine with liquid water (H_2O) in the ice and snow. This lowers the freezing point of the water, causing snow and ice to melt.

Like other chlorine compounds, road salt must be used with caution. Road salt pollutes rivers, lakes, and even the oceans. Rain washes the road salt off the roads, and it eventually flows to the nearest body of water. Excessive amounts of road salt harms the plants and animals that live in the delicate water ecosystems. Lake Ontario, one of the five Great Lakes between the United States and Canada, is one body of water with high levels of chlorine from the road salt that flows into it after heavy rain. Both countries are working together to reduce the amount of road salt used on highways and roads near Lake Ontario.

Another chlorine compound, calcium chloride ($CaCl_2$), is also used to melt ice and snow. Calcium chloride is generally harmless to

Sodium chloride is also rock salt and is used to keep icy walks and streets clear in winter.

plants and soil. It can also be used to make the water in swimming pools "harder," meaning it increases water's mineral content. Water with higher mineral content can reduce the wear and tear on the pool's concrete.

Life with Chlorine

From the ozone layer to the oceans, the dangers of chlorine compounds seem to be everywhere. However, chlorine is also at work inside your stomach, and it is a major reason why you will probably never get sick from water-borne bacteria. You can swim without concern of getting sick!

From industry and manufacturing to food preparation and water decontamination, the benefits of chlorine and its compounds guarantee that the element will continue to be used for a long time.

Glossary

atom Smallest, most basic unit of an element, made up of protons, neutrons, and electrons.

atomic number Number of protons in the nucleus of an atom.

atomic weight Average mass of one atom of an element.

bond Force that holds two things together.

compound Substance made up of two or more elements.

covalent bond Chemical bond created when atoms share electrons.

diatomic Consisting of two atoms.

electrolysis Chemical change caused by passing an electric charge through water or other nonmetal substance.

electron Negatively charged particle located outside the nucleus of an atom.

element Matter made up of one kind of atom.

halogens A family of elements, including fluorine, chlorine, bromine, iodine, and astatine.

isotope Atom of an element having the same number of protons but a different number of neutrons.

molecule Smallest particle of a substance that retains the properties of the substance and is composed of one or more atoms.

neutron Subatomic particle within the nucleus of an atom that has no charge; found in the nucleus of all elements except hydrogen.

nucleus Core of an atom, containing protons and—except in the case of hydrogen—neutrons.

pesticide Chemical used to kill pests, such as insects.

Further Reading

Books

Dingle, Adrian. *The Elements: A Tour of the Periodic Table*. London, UK: New Burlington Books, 2017.

McGuire, Michael J. *The Chlorine Revolution: Water Disinfection and the Fight to Save Lives*. Denver, CO: American Water Works Association, 2013.

Nordstrom, Brian. *The Smart Guide to Chemistry*. Norman, OK: Smart Guide Publications, Inc., 2014.

Turner, Tracey. *20 Weapons of War*. Mankato, MN: Smart Apple Media, an imprint of Black Rabbit Books, 2016.

Websites

Khan Academy

www.khanacademy.org/science/chemistry

Videos, activities, and more to learn more about chlorine and chemistry.

LiveScience

www.livescience.com/28988-chlorine.html

A top to bottom look at chlorine!

Royal Society of Chemistry

www.rsc.org/periodic-table/element/17/chlorine

The Royal Society of Chemistry breaks down the basics about chlorine.

Bibliography

Bentor, Yinon. "Periodic Table: Chlorine." 2006. http://www.chemicalelements.com/elements/cl.html.

Blaszczak-Boxe, Agata. "Facts About Chlorine." LiveScience, October 28, 2014. https://www.livescience.com/28988-chlorine.html.

British Broadcasting Corporation. "Historic Figures: Sir Humphry Davy." http://www.bbc.co.uk/history/historic_figures/davy_humphrey.shtml.

Chemical Heritage Foundation. "Humphry Davy." 2005. http://www.chemheritage.org/classroom/chemach/electrochem/davy.html.

Chlorine Chemistry. "Chlorine 101: A Workhorse Chemical." Retrieved January 04, 2018. https://chlorine.americanchemistry.com/Chlorine-101.

Chlorine Chemistry. "Chlorine Story." Retrieved January 04, 2018. https://chlorine.americanchemistry.com/Chlorine/What-is-Chlorine/Chlorine-Story.

Chlorine Chemistry. "Epibatidine: Natural Frog Poison with a Surprising Benefit to Humans." Retrieved January 04, 2018. https://chlorine.americanchemistry.com/Science-Center/Chlorine-Compound-of-the-Month-Library/Epibatidine-Natural-Frog-Poison-with-a-Surprising-Benefit-to-Humans.

Cobb, Cathy, and Monty L. Fetterolf. *The Joy of Chemistry: The Amazing Science of Familiar Things.* Amherst, NY: Prometheus Books, 2005.

Dawson, Simon. "Chlorine-Washed Chicken Q&A: Food Safety Expert Explains Why US Poultry Is Banned in the EU." *Independent*, December

13, 2017. http://www.independent.co.uk/life-style/health-and-families/chlorine-washed-chicken-qa-food-safety-expert-explains-why-us-poultry-is-banned-in-the-eu-a7875131.html.

"Discovery and Assignment of Elements with Atomic Numbers 113, 115, 117 and 118." International Union of Pure and Applied Chemistry, June 08, 2016. https://iupac.org/discovery-and-assignment-of-elements-with-atomic-numbers-113-115-117-and-118.

"Global Salt Production, 2016 | Statistic." Statista. Retrieved January 04, 2018. (https://www.statista.com/statistics/237162/worldwide-salt-production).

Kingston Technical Software. "Sir Humphry Davy." August 1999. Retrieved January 2018. http://www.corrosion-doctors.org/Biographies/DavyBio.htm.

Le Moyne College Department of Chemistry. "Carl Wilhelm Scheele," 1997. Retrieved January 2018. http://web.lemoyne.edu/~GIUNTA/scheele.html.

National Geographic. *National Geographic Field Guide to the Birds of North America. Fourth Edition*. Washington, DC: National Geographic Society, 2002.

Natural Resources Defense Council. "The Story of Silent Spring," 1997. Retrieved January 2018. http://www.nrdc.org/health/pesticides/hcarson.asp.

Newton, David E. *Chemical Elements from Carbon to Krypton, Volume 1, A–F*. Farmington Hills, MI: The Gale Group, 1999.

Sharp, Tim. "Facts About Moscovium (Element 115)." LiveScience, December 01, 2016. https://www.livescience.com/41424-facts-about-ununpentium.html.

Sharp, Tim. "Facts About Nihonium (Element 113)." LiveScience, December 01, 2016. https://www.livescience.com/41416-facts-about-ununtrium.html.

Stwertka, Albert. *A Guide to the Elements*, Second Edition. New York, NY: Oxford University Press, Inc. 2002.

US Fish and Wildlife Service. "The Bald Eagle Is Back!" 2000. Retrieved January 2018. http://www.fws.gov/r9extaff/eaglejuly2.html.

Williams, Linda D. *Chemistry Demystified*. New York, NY: McGraw-Hill, 2003.

Wong, Edward. "As Trial Begins, Poison Attack Haunts Kurds." *New York Times,* August 21, 2006. https://www.nytimes.com/2006/08/21/world/middleeast/as-trial-begins-poison-attack-haunts-kurds.html.

Index